For Mimi
December 15, 2017
I love You!
-Mommy ◡ ♡

# Nadia
## The Girl Who Couldn't Sit Still

*By* Karlin Gray

*Illustrated by* Christine Davenier

HOUGHTON MIFFLIN HARCOURT
Boston   New York

In the village of Onești, Romania, a country rich with forests and mountains, there lived a girl who couldn't sit still. She loved soccer, swimming, playing with dolls, and climbing trees. But she didn't just *climb* the trees—she swung from branch to branch until her family would call her home: "Nadia!"

Nadia Comaneci was a feisty and fearless little girl.
Once she got into trouble for trying on a pair of roller
skates in a store . . . and skating right out of the building.

Another time, she couldn't wait
for her father to tighten the screws
on her new bicycle . . . and it fell
apart as she rode away.

And one year, she climbed up the Christmas tree to eat the candies dangling from the top . . . and ended up underneath the fallen tree.

"Nadia, why on earth do you spend all your time climbing trees?" her grandmother asked her.

Nadia answered simply, "Because they are here to be climbed."

To find a place for all that energy, Nadia's mother signed her up for gymnastics lessons. When Nadia stepped into the gym, she felt a little overwhelmed by the big space and strange equipment. But she also saw plenty of room to jump, swing, and run!

At school recess, Nadia and her friend loved to cartwheel their way around the playground. A gymnastics coach named Bela Karolyi spotted them. Bela and his wife, Marta, asked the girls to join their new gymnastics school. Nadia's parents agreed.

Six-year-old Nadia liked her math and science classes at the new school, but she loved gymnastics best.

Bela and Marta taught her how to do a straight cartwheel on a line painted on the floor . . .

then on a low balance beam surrounded by cushions . . .

and finally on the high balance beam.

Nadia practiced all her skills until she mastered them and moved on to learning more difficult moves. Soon, Nadia was flying from bar to bar, from floor to vault, and high above the beam.

When she was nine, Nadia traveled with Bela's team to her first National Junior Championships competition. After so much hard work and practice, Nadia had perfected her routines. But when she did a leap on the beam, Nadia fell.

Angry and embarrassed, she tried again and fell again. With her ears burning, she tried a third time and fell for the third time. Nadia finished in thirteenth place.

Disappointed but determined, Nadia continued to practice for many hours each day.

And at the next National Junior Championships games, she won first place.

Nadia kept improving and competing, practicing and perfecting, until she reached the highest competition . . .

# . . . the Olympic Games!

In Montreal, Canada, the best gymnasts from all over the world—including the Russian gold medalists from the previous Olympics, Olga Korbut and Lyudmila Turischeva—were ready to compete. Judges scored each athlete's performance on a ratings system from 1 (a terrible score) to 10 (a perfect score).

"You all know what to do," Bela instructed his team. "Remember what we practiced and make yourselves and your country proud."

Then, over the loudspeaker: "Now entering the arena for the 1976 Olympic Games, the Romanian team!"

On the first day of the competition, Nadia's team performed on the beam, floor, and vault. Nadia scored a 9.9, 9.75, and 9.7 on these events. Next, the Romanians took their turn at the bars, where Olga had scored a 9.9.

Nadia mounted the bars. Now fourteen years old, she was a long way from the forests in Romania. But she swung around as easily as she had jumped from branch to branch as a little girl. The audience gasped as she twirled and whipped and flipped.

Nadia finished her routine by soaring through the air and landing perfectly on the mat below. The crowd exploded with applause.

After a long wait, the scoreboard flashed a number: 1.00. A terrible score.

Nadia looked at Bela. Bela looked at the judges. The crowd watched in confused silence.

"What is Nadia's score?" Bela asked.

One of the officials held up ten fingers as a voice announced over the loudspeaker: "Ladies and gentlemen, for the very first time in Olympic history, Nadia Comaneci has received the score of a perfect ten!"

The scoreboard had been programmed with only enough space to go as high as 9.99 because no male or female gymnast had ever received a 10.00.

Nadia turned to Bela. "Is that really a ten?"

"You bet it is, Nadia." Bela smiled and the audience went wild, clapping and cheering.

But the competition was not over, so Nadia moved on to her next event and her next perfect 10!

Again and again, Nadia's scores were
perfect. When the competition ended,
she had earned seven perfect 10s.

At the medal ceremonies, Olga and Lyudmila congratulated the new Olympic champion.

Nadia won five Olympic medals (three gold, one silver, and one bronze) and became the youngest Olympic gold medalist in gymnastics ever.

Reporters surrounded Nadia with questions. One asked her how it felt having the world's attention. "I feel just the same as before," she answered. One asked her if she had been confident she would win. "Yes. I was sure," Nadia said. And one reporter asked her when would she retire. "Retire?" she replied. "I'm fourteen years old."

When Nadia returned home, thousands of cheering Romanians, including the president of Romania, greeted her and her teammates.

Now famous around the world, Nadia went back to Oneşti—back to her family, her school, and her gym, where she could fly from bar to bar, from floor to vault, and high above the beam.

Even with all her achievements and medals, she continued to practice and aim for perfection. After all, Nadia was a girl who wouldn't sit still.

# Afterword

In fact, Nadia did not stay still. Four years later, she competed in the next Olympics, winning gold. And later, she worked as a gymnastics coach, teaching young girls the sport she loved so much. But when the government restricted Nadia's movement by not allowing her to travel, she decided to defect—to escape and leave her country.

Moving with a small team of defectors, Nadia walked through icy rivers and climbed over barbed-wired fences to get to the border. When the group crossed into Hungary, guards recognized the famous gymnast. They said she could stay but that the others would be sent back to Romania. Nadia refused. "We came together, we stay together." The guards eventually agreed and all were allowed to stay. In the next few years Nadia made her way to the United States, where she lives and works today.

## Timeline

**November 12, 1961:** Nadia Elena Comaneci (last syllable rhymes with "peach") is born.

**1967:** Nadia begins training with Bela and Marta Karolyi.

**1969:** At Nadia's first Romanian National Junior Championships, she comes in thirteenth place.

**1970:** At Nadia's second Romanian National Junior Championships, she wins gold.

**1975:** At the European Championships, Nadia wins four gold medals (all-around, bars, beam, and vault) and one silver medal (floor).

**1976:** At the American Cup, Nadia is the women's champion.

**1976:** At the Olympics in Montreal, Canada, Nadia earns seven perfect 10s, three gold medals (all-around, beam, bars), one silver (team), and one bronze (floor). She becomes the youngest all-around Olympic gold medalist ever.

**1977:** At the European Championships, Nadia wins two gold medals (overall, bars) and one silver (vault).

**1978:** At the World Championships, Nadia wins gold (beam) and two silver medals (vault and team).

**1979**: At the European Championships, Nadia wins gold (all-around, vault, and floor) and bronze (beam).

**1980:** At the Moscow Olympics, Nadia wins two gold medals (beam and floor) and two silver medals (all-around and team).

**1989:** Nadia defects from Romania.

**1993:** Nadia is inducted into the International Gymnastics Hall of Fame.

**1996:** Nadia marries her friend and fellow Olympic champion Bart Conner. Together they run the Bart Conner Gymnastics Academy in Norman, Oklahoma.

**2003:** *Letters to a Young Gymnast* by Nadia Comaneci is published.

**2006:** The International Gymnastics Federation changes gymnastics scoring from the perfect 10 system to a more complicated one by which top scores range from 15 to 17.

## Notes

"Nadia, why on earth . . ." Comaneci and Smither, *Nadia*, p.29.

"You all know what to do . . ." Karolyi and Richardson, *Feel No Fear,* p. 59.

"Now entering the arena . . ." Ibid., p. 60.

"Ladies and gentlemen . . ." Ibid., p. 61.

"What is Nadia's score?" Ibid., p. 61.

"Is that really a ten?" Ibid., p. 61.

"You bet is is, Nadia." Ibid., p. 61.

"I feel just the same as before . . ." Schreiber, "The Games," p. 47.

"Yes. I was sure . . ." Axthelm, "Olympics '76," p. 60.

"Retire? . . ." Bonventre, "Princess of the Games," p. 68.

"A Star Is Born" Axthelm, "Olympics '76"; "She Stole the Show" Deford, "Nadia Awed Ya";
  "She's Perfect" Schreiber, "The Games."

"We came together . . ." Comaneci, *Letters to a Young Gymnast,* p. 175.

*Selected Bibliography*

Anderson, Dave. "Nadia Comaneci: The Perfect 10." *New York Times,* July 21, 1976.

Axthelm, Pete. "Olympics '76: A Star Is Born." *Newsweek,* August 2, 1976.

Bonventre, Peter. "Princess of the Games." *Newsweek,* August 2, 1976.

Comaneci, Nadia. *Letters to a Young Gymnast.* New York: Basic Books, 2004.

Comaneci, Nadia, and Graham Buxton Smither. *Nadia: The Illustrated Autobiography of Nadia Comaneci.* New York:
  Proteus Books, 1981.

Deford, Frank. "Nadia Awed Ya." *Sports Illustrated,* August 2, 1976.

Gutman, Dan. *Gymnastics.* New York: Viking, 1996.

Karolyi, Bela, and Nancy Ann Richardson. *Feel No Fear: The Power, Passion, and Politics of a Life in Gymnastics.*
  New York: Hyperion, 1994.

Schreiber, LeAnne. "The Games: Up in the Air." *Time,* August 2, 1976.

*Websites*

CNN, "Human to Hero: Nadia Comaneci–Olympic gymnastics' first perfect 10": edition.cnn.com/2012/04/03/sport
  /olympics-nadia-comaneci/index.html

Official website of the Olympic Games: www.olympic.org/nadia-comaneci

Official website of Nadia Comaneci: bartandnadia.com

Official website of the International Gymnastics Hall of Fame: www.ighof.com/honorees/1993_Nadia_Comaneci.php

The Olympic Studies Center: www.olympic.org/olympic-studies-centre

*For Mom, Dad, Jeff, and Gabriel* —K.G.

*For my dear dad, Pierre Davenier, who tried desperately to teach me how to*

*do a cartwheel!* —C.D.

Text copyright © 2016 by Karlin Gray
Illustrations copyright © 2016 by Christine Davenier

All rights reserved. For information about permission to reproduce selections from this book,
write to trade.permissions@hmhco.com or to Permissions, Houghton Mifflin Harcourt
Publishing Company, 3 Park Avenue, 19th Floor, New York, New York 10016.

www.hmhco.com

The text of this book is set in Calisto MT.

The art was created using Ecoline and Colorex ink, and colored pencil, on Keaykolour paper.
Library of Congress Cataloging-in-Publication Control Number 2014048562
ISBN 978-0-544-31960-8

Manufactured in Malaysia
TWP 10 9 8 7 6 5 4 3
4500652833

*As a girl, Nadia collected more than two hundred dolls and often brought one to her gymnastic meets. When she was an adult, her foundation created a Nadia doll for "10 for Gymnastics"—a program that raised money for Romanian children's gymnastic clubs.*